Easy Soup Recipes
Love of Cooking
Maggie & Brooke

Legal Disclaimers and Notices
Easy Soup Recipes
Copyright 2012

Introduction

Hi Cooking Lovers,

We have gathered a wonderful collection of Soups, Stews & Chili for you. We are so very glad to share our recipes with you! We have been trying out recipes all of our lives. We love to find new ones to share with friends & family. Many of these have actually come from friends & family members. It is so much fun to find a recipe & add or even subtract ingredients for a whole new dish. Some people might tell you to FOLLOW THE RECIPE, but we want you to get in that kitchen & play. Give a dish your own style & taste (not to say that we haven´t made them exceptional).

Now, **Start Cooking & Enjoy!**

Visit us on our website: LoveofCookingOnline.com
Check out our Books:

Love of Cooking: Volume I:
Amazing Appetizer Recipes
Amazing Side Dish Recipes
Simple Salad Recipes
Easy Soup Recipes
Marvelous Main Dishes

Love of Cooking: Volume II:
Easy Chicken Recipes
Simple Beef Recipes

Love of Cooking: Holiday Series:
Love of Cooking: 4th of July
Love of Cooking: Labor Day
Thanksgiving Recipes
Easy Christmas Recipes Maggie & Brooke

**Get 5 bonus desert recipes!
Just use your computer and type**
http://www.VelocityHouseCooking.com/soups
**into your browser for
free instant access**

Table of Contents

SOUPS/HOT

The title of this section seems a little redundant, doesn´t it? Well there really are some soups that aren´t hot. These are hot soups that we have gathered to share with our readers to warm your tummy during the cool/cold weather. Soup especially hot soup just makes you feel better even if you feel pretty good already.
Enjoy!

Best Ever 15 Bean Soup

Start/Finish a couple of days

1 12oz pkg 15 bean soup
Water

1 32oz box of chicken broth w/water to make
   3qts.
1 lb ham bone
2 c ham, diced
1/2 tsp thyme
1 bay leaf
2 Tbsp parsley
2 tsp fish blackened seasoning

3 c onion, chopped
2 c celery, chopped
1 c carrots, sliced
1 bunch green onion, sliced
1 1/2 c chicken breast, diced
1 28oz can diced stewed tomatoes
3 cloves of garlic, crushed
Hot Pepper Sauce

1 lb Polish Sausage, sliced, browned & drained

2 c dry wine

Soak beans overnight, drain & rinse.

Place beans, broth thinned w/water, ham bone, ham, thyme, parsley & fish seasoning to 8 qt stockpot. Bring to a boil. Reduce heat & simmer 3 hrs.

Add onions, celery, carrots, green onions, chicken, tomatoes & garlic. Cover & simmer another 1 hr.

Stir often. Test for seasoning & add hot pepper sauce to taste.

Add sausage & wine. Simmer another 1 hr.

Refrigerate when cool for 12-24 hrs. Remove ham bone & strip off meat. Remove bay leaf. Reheat slowly. Stir often.

Ladle into bowls.

It's called Best Bean Soup for a reason. You will fall in love!

When we started to make this soup we gave it to a few friends. They told us it was the "Best" hence the name. Enjoy!

Serves 10-12

Cheesy Beer Soup

Start/Finish 25min

4 Tbsp butter
1 med onion, chopped
2 stalks of celery, chopped
2 med carrots, shredded

1/2 c flour (all purpose)

1 12oz bottle or can dark beer, flat
   (Belgian is best)
1 14 1/2 oz can chicken broth
1 bay leaf
Dash of white pepper

1 c half & half

3/4 lb cheddar cheese, shredded (3c)

Salt and cayenne pepper to taste.

Croutons

Melt butter in 3 qt saucepan. Add onion, garlic, celery & carrots. Sauté until onions are transparent but not brown. Sprinkle flour over mixture & stir until completely mixed.

Add beer & chicken broth bay leaf and white pepper. Bring to a boil, reduce heat, cover & simmer until veggies are tender (approx 15 min).

Heat over med-low heat until soup is steaming.

Add half & half stirring constantly. Do Not Boil. Add cheese, about 2 Tbsp at a time, whisking after each addition until cheese melts. Do Not Let Boil.

Season to taste w/salt & cayenne pepper.

Ladle into cups, crocks or soup bowls. Serve immediately.

Top w/ croutons.

As you may imagine, this is a guys favorite, but don't let them eat it all. Ladies love it too.

This is a pub recipe. In most pubs, they will have a beer cheese soup.

If you want to make it extra special: add 1 Tbsp of lump crab meat or sm cooked shrimp.

Serves 10

Chicken Taco Soup

Start/Finish 3hrs

4 chicken breasts
1 Tbsp seasoned salt
1 Tbsp coarse ground black pepper
1 Tbsp garlic powder

1 yellow onion, chopped
1 bell pepper, chopped
4 10 oz cans chicken broth or stock from boiled
   chicken
1 14 oz can diced stewed tomatoes
1 14 oz can "chili recipe" diced tomatoes
1 10 oz can tomatoes w/green chilies
1 15oz can black beans
1 15oz can pinto beans
1 14 1/2 oz can creamed corn
1 pkg taco seasoning
1 pkg ranch dressing, dry
1 tsp cumin
1 tsp garlic powder

Shredded cheddar cheese
Tortilla chips
Sour cream

Boil chicken breast in 6 qt stockpot with seasoned salt, black pepper & garlic powder for 2 hrs (until chicken is tender). Remove chicken from pot, de-bone & cut into bite sized pieces. Save stock.

Combine chicken & all remaining ingredients in stockpot. Simmer & stir occasionally for 1 hr to blend flavors. Top with cheese, chips & sour cream.

This is a great alternative to chili.

It is great on a cold day. Chicken, veggies, chili flavors all combined to make a hearty soup to warm your tummy.

Even better the next day. Great for potluck or game day.

Serves 8-10

Classic Chicken Noodle Soup

Start/Finish 2 hrs

1 whole chicken, cutup, Neck & back
  reserved
3 qts water
2 lg onions, cut into chunks
3 carrots, cut into chunks
3 stalks of celery w/leaves
2 cloves of garlic, minced
1 tsp salt
1/2 tsp pepper

1 bunch of parsley stems
1/3 c parsley leaves, chopped

2 cups egg noodles

Place chicken, including neck & back into 8 qt stockpot. Add water, onions, carrots, celery, garlic, salt & pepper. Bring to a boil. Cover partially. Reduce heat & simmer 1-2 hrs.

Remove chicken to plate. Remove carrots, celery & parsnips to bowl. Remove chicken from bone. Cut chicken into bite sized pieces. Return bones & skin to pot. Add parsley stems. Simmer 45min.

Strain broth. Retain stock & discard solids. Bring stock to a boil Add noodles to stock and cook according to package directions.

Add chicken & veggies to pot. Stir in parsley.

Just like your Mom made when you felt bad.

If this doesn't make you feel better nothing will.

Serves 8

Classic French Onion Soup

Start/Finish 1 hr 45min

4 or 5 lg white onions, sliced thin
3 Tbsp butter
1/4 tsp course ground black pepper

1 Tbsp flour (all purpose)

3 10 3/4 oz cans beef broth
3 c water
1 bay leaf

6-8 slices of French bread
2 Tbsp Parmesan cheese
1 c Gruyere or Swiss cheese, grated

Heat butter in a 4 qt saucepan. Add onions & pepper. Sauté mixture until golden brown.

Sprinkle flour over onion mixture. Stir until all traces of flour disappear. Cook 1 min longer, stirring constantly w/wooden spoon. Remove from heat.

Gradually add the beef broth to onion mixture, stir constantly. Stir in water & bay leaf. Return to med-high heat. Bring to a boil. Reduce heat, simmer uncovered for about 30 min. Discard bay leaf.

Season to taste.

Ladle soup into individual broil-proof bowls.

Toast bread. Place toast pieces on top of soup. Sprinkle toast w/cheese liberally. Place bowls 6 in from broiler. Broil until cheese is brown.

This can be a challenge to eat w/all the stringy cheese, but worth the battle.

Serves 6

Creamy Chicken & Wild Rice Soup

Start/Finish 30 min

2 skinless, boneless chicken breast
3 c chicken broth
1 c water

2 Tbsp butter
1 c celery, sliced
1/2 c carrots, shredded coarse
1/2 c onion, chopped
1/2 c green bell pepper, chopped

3 Tbsp flour (all purpose)
1 tsp salt
1/4 tsp pepper

1 1/2 c cooked wild rice

1 c half & half
1/3 c almonds, sliced & toasted
1/4 c parsley, chopped

Place chicken, broth & water in a 6 qt stockpot. Bring to a simmer. Cook the chicken thru 8-10 min.
Skim any scum. Remove chicken from broth. Let cool & cut into bite sized pieces. Reserve broth.

In pot, melt butter. Add celery, onion & green peppers. Cook until soft (approx 5 min).

Stir in flour, salt & pepper until blended.

Add cooked rice, chicken & broth. Stir to combine. Bring to a boil. Cover & reduce heat. Simmer for 15 min. Stir occasionally.

Add half & half, almonds & parsley.

Cook until hot. (Do Not Boil)

This is such a tasty soup.

You can use a wild rice mix (brown & wild) instead of plain wild rice. The mixes just add some flavor.

Serves 6

Extra Sharp
Broccoli Cheddar Soup

Start/Finish 25 min

2 Tbsp butter
3 Tbsp flour (all purpose)

4 c milk
3/4 tsp salt
1/2 tsp dry mustard
1/4 tsp cayenne pepper

1 10 oz pkg frozen chopped broccoli,
    thawed & drained
1/2 c red bell pepper, chopped fine

6 oz extra sharp cheddar cheese, shredded

Green onions, chopped

Melt butter in 6 qt stockpot. Add flour & cook until bubbling (approx 30 sec)

Add milk, salt, dry mustard & cayenne pepper. Bring to a boil. Reduce heat & simmer over high heat stirring frequently for 5 min.

Add broccoli & red pepper. Return to a boil. Reduce heat & simmer uncovered for 5 min. Stir occasionally.

Add cheese. Stir constantly over low heat just until cheese melts (do not boil).

Ladle into bowls. Top with green onions.

This would be a good way to get the kids to eat broccoli. I know I love cheese on my broccoli.

Take your time making this. If it boils the cheese could separate. It will not be good at all then.

Serves 4

Family Favorite
Loaded Baked Potato Soup

Start/Finish 1 hr10 min

4 lg baking potatoes

2/3 c butter
2/3 c flour
6 c milk

3/4 tsp salt
1/2 tsp pepper
4 green onions, chopped
12 slices of bacon, cooked & crumbled
1 1/4 c cheddar cheese
8 oz sour cream

Bake potatoes & scoop out meat.

Melt butter in a 3 qt saucepan & add flour. Cook 1 min, gradually adding milk. Cook until thick & bubbly (about 4 min).

Add potato pulp, salt & pepper, 2 Tbsp of green onions, half of the bacon & 1 c of cheese. Cook until heated. Stir in sour cream & add extra milk if needed.

Ladle into bowls & top with remaining onions, bacon & cheese.

As good as any loaded baked potato, maybe better.

My little girl loves this soup more than anything. She gets it when we go out to eat & loves this version too. Give it a try. It's delicious.

Serves 8-10

Fiery Black Bean Soup

Start/Finish 2 1/2 hrs (on cooking day)

1 lb dry black beans
Cold water

2 ham hocks

2 Tbsp olive oil
1 lg yellow onion, chopped
1 clove garlic, crushed

2 10 3/4 oz can of beef broth

4 tsp jalapenos, seeded & chopped
1 Tbsp chili powder
1 tsp cumin
1 tsp cayenne pepper
1 1/2 tsp salt
3/4 tsp ground black pepper

Cover beans with cold water. Soak overnight.

Drain beans. Cover with fresh water in a 6 qt stockpot. Add ham hocks. Bring to a boil. Reduce heat & simmer for 2 hrs. Drain beans & reserve stock.

Remove & debone ham hocks. Cut meat into chunks.

Place olive oil, garlic & onions in pot. Sauté veggies until brown. Deglaze pan w/1 can of beef broth.

Add beans, ham, jalapenos & spices.

Place beef broth in a lg measuring cup. Add reserved stock & water to make 5 cups. Add liquid to the pot. Bring to a boil. Cover & reduce heat. Simmer 10 min.

Ladle into soup bowls. Top with onions, sour cream & tortilla chips.

We like this over rice. It makes it a heartier soup. You can leave off the chips or keep them for the crunch.

Some people like to pour vinegar & oil on top.

Serves 10-12

Hearty Vegetable Beef Soup

Start/Finish 5 1/2 hrs

2 Tbsp olive oil
1 lb stew meat
1 soup bone (beef)
Seasoned Salt
Black pepper
Garlic powder

3 1/2 qts water
1 tsp oregano dried or 2 Tbsp fresh, chopped
1 tsp basil dried or 2 Tbsp fresh, chopped
1 tsp parsley flakes or 2 Tbsp fresh, chopped
1 Tbsp chili powder
2 tsp salt
2 tsp pepper

1 med green pepper, chopped
1 lg stalk of celery, chopped
2 lg yellow onions, chopped

1 28oz can diced stewed tomatoes
1 10oz can diced tomatoes w/green chilies
1 sm head cabbage, chopped
1 pkg frozen soup or gumbo veggies
1 pkg frozen stew veggies

Brown meat & soup bone seasoned with garlic powder, seasoned salt & pepper in olive oil in an 8 qt stockpot.

Add water & other spices. Add green pepper, onions & celery. Bring to a boil, reduce heat and simmer approx 4 hrs (until meat is tender & meat falls off the soup bone) remove meat & chop.

Add back to soup & add more water if necessary.

Add tomatoes, cabbage & frozen veggies. Cook about1 hr (until veggies are tender). Season to taste.

Best if cooked the day before serving to let the flavors blend. Refrigerate & reheat slowly.

Maggie gets carried away when she makes soup. All of her friends are delighted that it is soup day at Maggie's because that means there will be lots to share.

Serves 8 *if you can only eat 1 bowl*

Italian Sausage Soup

Start/Finish 30 min

8 oz sweet Italian pork sausage, sliced
8 oz hot Italian pork sausage, sliced

2 Tbsp olive oil
4 potatoes, sliced thin
1 red bell pepper, cut into strips
1 green bell pepper, cut into strips
1 red onion, cut into strips
4 cloves of garlic, minced
1 tsp oregano
1/2 tsp rosemary
4 c chicken broth
3/4 c tomato paste
1/4 c water

Green onions
Parmesan cheese
Croutons

Brown sausage in 8 qt stock pot. Remove sausage with slotted spoon, place in bowl. Discard pan drippings and wipe out with paper towel.

Heat oil in pot. Sauté potatoes, red & green peppers, onions, garlic oregano & rosemary for 5 min or until potatoes are tender

Stir in broth, tomato paste, 1/4 c water & sausage. Cover & cook for 10 min. Stir occasionally.

Season to taste.

Ladle into bowls. Top w/green onions, Parmesan cheese & croutons.

You may need a knife & fork.

Serves 8

Mama's Potato Soup

Start/Finish 45 min

6-8 baking potatoes, cubed

1 c celery, chopped fine
2 med onions, chopped fine
1 stick of butter
3/4 c flour

1 qt half & half or whole milk

Green onions, chopped fine

Cover potatoes with water in a 8 qt stockpot. Bring to a boil. Reduce heat & simmer until potatoes are fork tender (approx 30 min).

At the same time, melt butter in a sm skillet & then add celery, onions. Sauté until veggies are transparent.

Sprinkle flour over veggies & stir constantly until the flour disappears. Do Not Brown.

Stir roux into pot. Add half & half or milk. Stir constantly until slightly thickened.

Ladle into bowls & top with green onions.

This hearty soup makes a good substitute for chicken soup when you are feel bad. It's what our Mama gave us when we felt bad.

Serves 6-8

Minestrone Soup

Start/Finish 1 hr (on cooking day)

1 c dried navy beans
Water

2 10 3/4 oz can chicken broth
2 qt water
2 tsp salt

1 sm head of cabbage
4 carrots, peeled & sliced 1/4 in. thick
2 med potatoes, peeled & cut into 1/2 in. cubes

1 16 oz can Italian style tomatoes

2 med onions, chopped
1/4 c olive oil

1 celery stalk, sliced diagonally 1/8 in. thick
2 zucchinis, sliced 1/4 in thick
1 lg fresh tomato, peeled & cut into 1/2 cubes
1 clove garlic, crushed
1/4 tsp black pepper

1/4 c parsley, chopped
1 c thin spaghetti, broken

Soak beans overnight. Drain & place in 8 qt stockpot.

Place chicken broth in lg measuring cup. Add water to reach 1 qt. Pour over beans. Add 2 more qts of water & salt. Bring to a boil.
 Reduce heat & simmer covered 1hr. Chop cabbage, carrots & potatoes now.

Add prepared veggies & can tomatoes to beans. Cook 30 min. Prep the rest of the veggies now.

Add oil & onions to a med skillet. Sauté 5 min. Add remaining veggies, salt & pepper to onions.

Cook slowly, stirring occasionally for 20 min. Add to bean mixture.

Add parsley & spaghetti.

Cover & cook slowly, stirring occasionally for 30 min.

Serve hot topped w/pesto sauce or cold plain.

Now THAT'S Italian!

Serves 10

New Orleans Onion Soup

Start/Finish 40 min

> 1 1/2 c butter
> 4 c sliced white onions
>
> 1 3/4 c flour
>
> 12 c beef bouillon
> 1/2 tsp cayenne pepper
> 1 1/2 Tbsp salt
>
> 1 egg yolk
> 2 Tbsp cream
>
> Croutons
> Parmesan Cheese

Melt butter in a 6 qt stockpot. Reduce heat to very low.

Add onions. Cook until onions melt down, but make sure not to brown the onions.

Add flour & cook 10-15 min stirring occasionally.

Blend in bouillon, cayenne pepper & salt. Bring to a boil. Reduce heat & simmer for about 15 min.

Remove pot from heat.

Beat together egg yolk & cream. Add a little of the soup & mix quickly. Add mixture back to pot.

Fill individual oven safe bowls with soup. Top with croutons & Parmesan cheese. Place under broiler until brown.

You will feel like you are eating in the French Quarter

Serves 10-12

New Year's Day
Black Eyed Pea Soup

Start/Finish 3 1/2 hrs (on cooking day)

>2 c dried black eyed peas
>Water
>1 Tbsp Salt
>
>1 ham hock
>
>1 lg onion, chopped
>1 lb cooked ham, cubed
>1 10oz can tomatoes w/green chilies
>2 cloves garlic, crushed or 1/2 tsp minced garlic
>Juice of 1 lemon or 3-4 Tbsp of lemon juice

Wash peas, add salt & water (enough to cover peas). Let soak overnight.

Drain peas, cover with water in a 6 qt stockpot. Add ham hock & bring to a boil. Reduce heat. Boil gently for 3 hrs.

Add remaining ingredients and simmer for 30 min. Season to taste.

Perfect for a New Year's Day party. Help everyone out with their luck for the New Year.

Serve w/hot cornbread. Unbelievably great!

Serves 8

Old-Fashioned Butter Bean Soup

Start/Finish 1 hr 45 min (on cooking day)

1 lb dried extra large white lima beans
Water

1 smoked ham hock
1 28oz can of whole stewed tomatoes
3 c water
2 10 3/4 can of chicken broth
1/2 tsp paprika
Dash of cayenne pepper

2 or 3 stalks of celery
1 lg yellow onion

1 c smoked ham, cubed
1/4 c parsley, chopped

Place beans in a bowl. Add water, enough to cover beans. Soak beans overnight.

Drain & rinse beans. Discard liquid. Place beans in 10 qt stockpot. Add ham hock, the un-drained tomatoes, 3 c water, chicken broth, paprika & cayenne pepper.

Bring to a boil. Reduce heat & simmer for 30 min. Chop veggie's now (about 1c ea).

Add veggies to pot & stir to mix. Cover beans & simmer until beans are soft, but not mushy (approx 1 hr). Remove pot from heat. Remove ham hock & let cool.

Cut meat from ham hock & add to beans. Discard bone. Add ham cubes & parsley.

Reheat soup very slowly until hot stirring frequently.

Some people call these butter beans, others think of them as white lima beans, our family calls them "Big Willies." I have no idea why.

This soup is so comforting & hearty enough for a guy to fill up on.

Serves 10-12

Spicy Chicken Vegetable Soup
♥ MAG'S FAV

Start/Finish 3 hrs

3 chicken breast w/ribs
1 Tbsp seasoned salt
2 tsp black pepper
2 tsp garlic powder

1/2 head of green cabbage, cut into chunks
2 yellow onions, cut into chunks
2 bell peppers, cut into pieces
12 pieces of okra, cut into lg slices
5 carrots, cut into lg pieces
5 stalks of celery, cut into lg pieces
1 28oz can of diced stewed tomatoes
1 10oz can of diced tomatoes w/green chilies

Fill an 8 qt stockpot with water. Add chicken, seasoned salt, black pepper & garlic powder. Bring water to a boil. Reduce slightly and boil for 2 hrs (until meat is tender). Chop veggies now.

Drain, saving stock, debone chicken & cut the chicken into chunks.

Replace the stock & chicken into pot. Add water if needed to cover everything. Add all veggies including the tomatoes. Bring to a boil.

Reduce heat & simmer for about 45 min (until veggies are tender).

This soup has a kick, but you can spice it up even more with the hot version of the tomatoes w/green chiles.

We make this soup almost every Monday & eat on it all week while we work.

Serves 8-10

Steak Soup

Start/Finish 1 1/2 hrs

    1 lb ground sirloin
    1 c onion, chopped

    1 1/2 qt water
    3/4 c potato, chopped
    1 c carrots, sliced
    1/2 c celery, chopped
    1 c cabbage, shredded
    1 8 oz can tomato sauce
    1/4 c rice

    1 leaf of sweet basil, crumbled or 1/2 T dried
    3 tsp salt
    Dash of pepper
    1 sm bay leaf
    1/2 tsp thyme

Brown sirloin & onion in 6 qt stockpot. Drain fat. Return to pot.

Add water & all the veggies. Bring to a boil. Sprinkle rice into the mixture.

Add remaining spices. Cover & simmer for 1 hr.

This is so very filling. Great 1 pot meal.

This recipe came from Maggie & Tim's friend Colleen. She makes is when they play Bridge. Delicious!!

Easily doubled.

Serves 4-6

Taco Soup

Start/Finish 30 min

2 14 1/2 oz cans Mexican Style Stewed
    Tomatoes
1 10 oz can of stewed tomatoes w/green chilies
2 11 oz can Mexican corn
1 11 oz can of shoe peg corn
1 15oz can chili beans
1 15 oz can black beans

2 lbs ground beef, browned
1 onions, chopped

1 pkg ranch dressing (dry)
1 pkg taco seasoning

Place all canned veggie into an 8 qt stockpot. Heat to a boil. Reduce heat & simmer.

Brown beef & onions in a med skillet.

Add beef, onions, dressing & taco mix to veggie mixture. Return to a boil.

Reduce heat & simmer for 15 min to blend spices.

Excellent over tortilla chips or corn chips or serve with flour tortillas. Yummy!

Great for Pot Luck or instead of Chili. Even better the next day. This is a hit w/anyone that loves Tex/Mex.

Serves 8-10

Texas Tortilla Soup

Start/Finish 2 hrs 45 min

1 3 lb chicken
10 c water
2 onions, cut in half
6 stalks of celery, cut in half
8 sprigs of cilantro
4 chicken bouillon cubes

12 corn tortillas, torn
2 jalapenos, seeded & chopped
2 cloves of garlic

Tortilla chips
Shredded cheddar/jack cheese
Fresh cilantro, chopped

Rinse chicken. Combine chicken, water, onions, celery, cilantro & bouillon in an 8 qt stockpot. Bring to a boil. Reduce heat & simmer for 2 hr (until chicken is tender).

Drain, reserving stock & chicken.

Discard veggies.

Debone & shred chicken.

Place 2 c of reserved stock, tortillas, jalapenos & garlic in food processor & puree.

Add mixture & chicken to remaining stock. Simmer over low heat for 30 min or slightly thickened.

Stir occasionally.

Ladle into soup bowls. Top with chips, cheese & cilantro.

This started in Texas, but now it is popular all over the country. You can find a version of tortilla soup in just about any good Mexican restaurant.

Make it at home…it's always better!

Serves 6-8

Tomato-Basil Soup

Start/Finish 45 min

1/4 c butter
1 med onion, sliced
1 med leek, chopped fine
2 med carrots, chopped fine
1 med stalk of celery, chopped fine
2 Tbsp fresh parsley, chopped
2 Tbsp fresh basil, chopped or 2 tsp dried

4 lg ripe tomatoes, chopped
3 Tbsp tomato paste

2 Tbsp flour
1 1/2 c chicken broth

1/3 cup half & half

Melt butter in 8 qt stockpot over low heat. Add onion, leek, carrots, celery, parsley & basil. Sauté 5 min. Stir occasionally.

Add tomatoes & tomato paste. Continue cooking another 5 min.

Add flour & mix well. Add chicken broth. Bring to a boil. Reduce heat & simmer, covered, 20 min. Transfer 1/2 soup to food processor or blender & puree.

Return soup to pot. Add half & half. Bring soup to a boil. Reduce heat & simmer for 2 min. Season to taste.

Ladle into bowls. Garnish w/basil leaves. May also be served cold.

Also good if you add slices of cooked Italian sausage.

Husband Tim's favorite. He loves it in a restaurant, but prefers this one.

This takes a little time & effort, but so worth it.

Serves 4-6

Vegetarian Bean Soup

Start/Finish 20 min

2 14 1/2 oz can vegetable broth
1 c water

1 16 oz frozen mixed vegetables
1 14 1/2 oz can stewed tomatoes
1/3 c angel hair pasta, broken into 1-2 in
lengths

1 15oz can kidney beans
1 15oz can black beans
1 tsp Italian seasoning
1/2 tsp garlic powder

1/4 c Parmesan cheese

Pour broth & water into a 4 qt saucepan. Place over high heat.

While liquid is heating, add frozen veggies, tomatoes and pasta. Cover & bring to a boil. When it comes to a boil, uncover & stir well (you may need to scrape the bottom w/a wooden spoon to loosen stuck pasta.)

At the same time, rinse & strain beans. Add beans, Italian seasoning & garlic to pan. Reduce heat to med, maintaining moderate boil. Cook until pasta is tender (approx 5 min). Stir frequently.

Reduce the heat to low & add Parmesan cheese. Simmer for 5 min. Stir occasionally.

Ladle into soup bowls

This is delicious for everyone not just Vegetarians.

If you happen to want meat, you can add cooked chicken or ham.

This is a good side dish as well.

Serves 8

Yummy Split Pea Soup

Start/Finish 1 1/2 hrs (on cooking day)

1 12oz pkg split peas
Water
2 1/2 c water
1 c ham, diced
1 c celery, chopped
1 c onion, chopped
1/4 c green bell pepper, chopped

1 c milk
1 tsp salt
1/2 tsp pepper
Dash of celery salt
1 tsp Worcestershire sauce
2 Tbsp butter

Soak peas overnight. Drain & rinse.

Add fresh water to peas in a 6 qt stockpot. Bring to a boil. Reduce heat & simmer until peas are tender (approx 45 min).

Place ham, onion, celery, green peppers & 2 1/2 c water. Bring to a boil. Reduce heat & simmer until veggies are tender (approx 15-20 min).

Put peas (a sm batch at a time) in a blender or food processor & puree. Add pea puree to pot w/ham mixture.

Add milk, salt, pepper, celery salt, Worcestershire sauce & butter. Stir until combined.
Ladle into bowls.

I know pea soup sounds yucky to some people, but this is great. Give it a try.

Serves 10

SOUPS/COLD

Many people have never even
tried a cold soup. If you have
tried them you know that they
can be sweet or savory,
tangy or spicy. If you haven´t
tried them, now is the time.
We have given you a few to test out.
We know that you will
have a pleasant surprise.
Enjoy!

Chilled Strawberry Soup

Start/Finish 4 1/2 hrs

> 5 c fresh strawberries, sliced
>
> 2 1/2 c orange juice, fresh squeeze
> 1/2 c + 1 tsp orange brandy liqueur
>
> 1 Tbsp sour cream
> 1/2 c whipping cream
>
> 2 tsp sugar
>
> 6 strawberries
> 6 sprigs of mint

Place sliced strawberries in a blender or food processor until pureed.

Combine strawberry puree & orange juice & liqueur. Whisk until blended.

Beat whipping cream until it peaks. Fold in sour cream.

Chill, covered for 4 hrs. Stir in sugar.

Spoon into chilled dessert cups or chilled wine glasses. Top with strawberry & sprig of mint.

Serves 6

Chilly Potato Vichyssoise

Start/Finish 1hr

> 2 c green onions, sliced thin
> 1 c white onions, sliced thin
> 1/4 c butter
>
> 6 c chicken broth
> 5 1/2 c potatoes, sliced thin
> 1 Tbsp salt
> 1/2 c celery, chopped
>
> 1 qt half & half
> 3 c milk
>
> Chives, chopped

Sauté green & white onions in butter in a 4 qt saucepan until slightly transparent.

Add the chicken broth, potatoes, salt & celery. Bring to a boil, cover & cook until potatoes are very soft (approx 45 min).

Put into blender in sm batches adding milk gradually.

When mixture is very smooth, add half & half & mix well.

Pour all of the mixture into a bowl & chill very well.

Ladle into bowls & top with chives.

An elegant soup to serve on a warm day.

Serves 12

Cold Cranberry Soup

Start/Finish 1 1/2 hrs

2 oranges, juice & rind
1 Tbsp butter

1 1/4 c sugar
1 c sherry

1 lb cranberries, fresh or frozen

1 c dry white wine
1 c light cream
1 c sour cream

1 c club soda (optional)

Peel orange & cut rind into very fine julienne pieces.

Melt butter in 3 qt saucepan. Do Not Brown. Sauté rind.

Add sugar, sherry & orange juice. Boil 2 min.

Add cranberries & cover. Boil 2 min. Uncover & boil 3 more min.

Pour into a bowl. Chill for about 1 hr. Can be done in advance.

Put cranberry mixture in a food processor or blender.

Add wine. Blend 1 min. Add light cream & sour cream. Blend on med 1 min more.

Chill again. Add chilled club soda before serving. Mix well.

Pour into chilled wine glasses. This looks beautiful on your table.

This is sweet & tangy & could be a yummy dessert.

Serves 8-10

Easy White Gazpacho

Start/Finish 15 min

    2 med cucumbers, peeled & diced
    1 clove garlic
    3 c chicken broth

    2 c sour cream
    1 c plain yogurt
    3 tsp white vinegar
    2 tsp salt
    1/2 tsp pepper
    Green onions, chopped

Place cucumbers, garlic & 1 c of broth into blender or food processor. Blend to puree.

Add remaining broth. Slowly add remaining ingredients. Blend well.

Chill.

Another soup that looks beautiful in a wine glass.

Pour into chilled wine glasses & top with green onions.

Serves 4

54

Elegant Avocado Cream Soup

Start/Finish 20min

> 3 black Haas avocados,peeled and sliced
> 1 clove garlic, crushed
> 2 2/3 cups chicken broth
> 1/2 c heavy cream
>
> 1 Tbsp sour cream
> 1/4 c dry white wine
> Juice of 1/2 lemon or 2 Tbsp lemon juice
> Pinch of cayenne pepper
> 1/2 tsp salt
> 1/2 tsp white pepper
>
> Croutons
> 1 hard-boiled egg, chopped

Place avocado, garlic, chicken broth, heavy cream & sour cream in blender. Blend at low speed for 1 min.

Add wine, lemon juice & spices. Blend on high speed for 30 sec or until smooth.

Chill well.

Pour soup into 6 wine glassed. Top with croutons & hard-boiled egg.

For a fancier touch add a spoonful of lump crab meat instead of eggs.

Serves 6

Spicy Summer Gazpacho
♥ MAG'S FAV

Start/Finish 1 hr 15 min

4 med tomatoes, cut into chunks
1 lg cucumber, quartered
1 med onion, cut into chunks
1 green bell pepper, cut into chunks

1 lg bottle tomato/vegetable juice, chilled
1 Tbsp parsley, minced
1 lemon, juiced 3-4 Tbsp
1 clove garlic, cut in half
1 tsp celery seeds
1 tsp seasoned salt
1/2 tsp coarse ground pepper
1 1/2 tsp Worcestershire sauce
Hot sauce to taste
1 Tbsp olive oil

Croutons
Sour cream

Place tomatoes, cucumbers, onion & pepper in a food processor. Pulse to chop. (do not make it too juicy).

Add juice & spices Worcestershire, hot sauce & oil.

Pulse to desired texture.

Place in a large pitcher & chill well (at least 1 hr).

Pour into cups. Top with croutons & sour cream if desired

Makes a great Bloody Mary. Just add Vodka!

It seemed funny to my friends that I liked this as a kid, but I always loved it when my mom made it for a party. I discovered the Bloody Mary thing much later.

Serves 10

STEWS

The word Stew just feels hearty.
We found & (we feel) improved
on some already wonderful stews.
Creating your own Stew
is often times a great way
to clean out the frig. Don´t
forget that you can start with
a good solid recipe &
add your own twist.
Enjoy!

Country Pork Stew

Start/Finish 2 1/2hrs

6 carrots, cut into med chunks
2 stalks of celery, cut into med chunks
1 lg onion, cut into med chunks
4 Tbsp olive oil

1 1/2 boneless pork loin, cut into 2 in pieces
(you can ask the butcher)
3 sweet Italian sausage links, cut in half

1/2 tsp salt
Pinch of ground black pepper
1 bay leaf
2 Tbsp flour (all purpose)
1 c water
1 c white wine

Heat oil in 6 qt stockpot. Add veggies & sauté for 5 min. With slotted spoon remove veggies & set aside.

Brown pork pieces & sausage in remaining oil until well browned on all sides (approx 20 min).

Add salt, pepper, bay leaf & flour to the pot. Mix well. Add water & wine. Bring mixture to a boil.

Reduce heat & simmer until pork is fork tender (approx 1 1/2 hrs.). Add veggies for the last 1/2 hr.

Stir until well combined.

Delicious when served with boiled cabbage wedges & biscuits.

Serves 8

Dilly Veal Stew

Start/Finish 8hrs

1 1/4 lbs Veal Shoulder, cut up for stew
    (or ask the butcher)
1 Tbsp olive oil

12 pearl onions
1 14 1/2 can diced stewed tomatoes
8 oz bag baby carrots
1/4 c dry white wine (optional)
1/2 tsp pepper
1/2 tsp garlic, minced

1 10 3/4 oz can cream of mushroom soup

8 oz mushrooms, sliced

1/4 c fresh dill, chopped

1 pkg egg noodles, cooked & rinsed

Heat oil in med frying pan. Brown meat. Mix all ingredients (including browned meat) except mushroom soup, mushrooms & dill in a 4qt or bigger crock pot.

Cover & cook on low 7-9 hrs or until veal & veggies are done.

Stir in soup until blended. Add mushrooms. Recover & cook on high until mushrooms are tender (approx 15 min).

Cook noodles now.

Stir in Dill & serve.

Plate cooked egg noodles & spoon on stew.

Writing this recipe makes me hungry for this. I think I will make it tonight.

Serves 6

Elegant Oyster Stew

Start/Finish 25 min

4 Tbsp butter
1 tsp olive oil
1 med onion, chopped
2 shallots, chopped (optional)

2 Tbsp flour (all purpose)

1 tsp salt
1/2 tsp white pepper
1/2 c heavy cream
1 8 oz bottle of clam juice

1/4 c white wine (for thinner soup)

1 Tbsp fresh thyme or chives, or 1 1/2 tsp dried
1 pt oysters

Parsley, minced
4 1/2 tsp butter

In 8 qt stockpot melt butter & add oil on med- high heat. Add onions & shallots. Cook until soft, but not brown (approx 3 min)

Add flour to make a light roux. Cook 3-5 min, stirring constantly, but do not brown.

Add salt, white pepper, cream & clam juice. If you want thinner soup, add the white wine. Reduce heat to med & simmer until slightly thickened (approx 10 min).

Add thyme or chives & oysters. Cook oysters just until edges are curled (approx 1 min).

Ladle into bowls. Top w/parsley & pat of butter.

If you are a fan of oysters, you must give this a try. It is a whole new way to eat oysters.

Impress your guests with this recipe.

Serves 4

Flemish Drunken Beef Stew

Start/Finish 2hrs

4 lbs lean boneless beef stew meat
1/2 c flour (all purpose)
1 tsp salt
1/2 tsp black pepper

1/4 c butter

1 lb pearl onions, peeled

2 12oz dark beer (Belgian is best)
2 or 3 sprigs of fresh thyme or 1 tsp dried
2 bay leaves

2 tsp Dijon mustard
1 1/2 Tbsp red currant jelly or brown sugar
1 Tbsp red wine vinegar

1 8 oz pkg. wide egg noodles

Season the beef cubes w/salt & pepper, dredge in flour. Shake off excess flour.

Melt 2 Tbsp butter in lg heavy skillet until hot but not steaming. Add beef in batches. Sauté until brown on all sides. Add more butter if needed.

Transfer beef to heavy Dutch oven or oven proof casserole dish.

Add other 2 Tbsp butter to skillet. Add onions & brown. You may raise the heat to get an even brown surface on the onions.

Stir onions just enough to avoid burning. Add onions to beef.

Pour beer in skillet to deglaze, scraping w/wooden spoon to loosen and brown bits & bring to boil.

Pour beer from skillet over meat in Dutch oven.

Add thyme & bay leaves. Bring to boil, reduce heat & simmer, covered over low heat until meat is tender (approx 1 1/2 - 2 hrs). Just before serving, add mustard, jelly or brown sugar & vinegar.

Simmer 5 min.

Cook noodles now per pkg directions. Plate noodles & spoon stew over them.

Just like in a Belgian Pub.

Serves 8

Golden Potato & Beef Stew

Start/Finish 2 hrs 15 min

> 2 lbs stew meat
> 2 Tbsp vegetable oil
>
> 8-10 oz jar of horseradish
> 4 c beef stock
>
> 1 tsp black pepper
> Water
>
> 4 gold potatoes, sliced
> Salt to taste
>
> 3 c sour cream
> Dill weed

Brown meat in a 6 qt stockpot. Add horseradish, stock, pepper & water.

Bring to a boil. Reduce heat & simmer until meat is tender (approx 1 1/2 hrs.)

At the same time add potatoes to another 6 qt stockpot add salt. Bring to a boil & cook until potatoes are tender (approx 30 min).

Remove meat from heat. Let cool slightly. Add cooked potatoes & gently stir in sour cream.

Ladle into bowls & top with dill.

This is so creamy & delicious. The tender potatoes & dill are a perfect mix.

Great one dish meal.

Serves 6

Goulash

Start/Finish 2 1/2 hrs

> 3 Tbsp vegetable oil
> 1 lb lean beef stew meat
>
> 1 tsp Hungarian paprika
>
> 2 med onions, minced (1 1/2 c)
>
> 6 c chicken broth
>
> 3 carrots, sliced thin
> 4 med red potatoes, cubed
> 1 lg tomato, peeled & cut into 8ths
> 1/4 c parsley, chopped
> 1/2 tsp caraway seeds
> Salt & pepper to taste
> 1 bay leaf
> 1/4 tsp dried dill

Heat oil in 6 qt stockpot. Sauté beef until brown on all sides (approx 5min). Sprinkle in paprika &then remove meat with a slotted spoon.

Sauté onions in pot until they are soft, but not brown (approx 6-8 min).

Add broth & raise heat. When it simmers add meat. Cover & simmer until beef is tender (approx 2hrs).

Add carrots, potatoes, tomato, parsley & caraway seeds, bay leaf & dill. Season to taste. Cover & simmer until potatoes are fork tender (approx 15min). Remove bay leaf. Ladle into bowls.

You may want to add your favorite dumplings for a heartier soup. Add them in about 15 min. before serving.

Serves 6

Gumboo Z'Herbes (Green Gumbo)

Start/Finish 2 1/2 hrs

1 1/2 lbs beef smoked sausage, sliced in rings

1/2 c vegetable oil
1/2 c flour

2 c onions, chopped
2 c celery, chopped
1/2 c green bell pepper, chopped
2 clove garlic, chopped

7 boxes frozen spinach
1 box frozen mustard greens
1box frozen collard greens
1 box frozen turnip greens
3 qts chicken broth
1 qt water
1 bay leaf

3 c cooked rice

Brown sausage rings in an 8 qt stockpot. Remove & set aside. (For a spicier version use andioulle)

In the same pot, heat oil & gradually add flour. Stir constantly until flour becomes light to mid brown color.

Add onion, celery, bell pepper & garlic. If mixture begins to stick, add 1 c water.

Cook, stirring constantly, until onion is almost transparent.

Add all of the greens, broth, water & bay leaf. Blend & simmer until all greens are well mixed.

Add sausage. Simmer, covered for 30 min.

Season to taste w/salt, black & cayenne peppers.

Cover & simmer 1 1/2 hrs. Stir occasionally.

Plate 1/4 c of rice into bowl & ladle gumbo over it.

Cajun food lovers will surely embrace this version of Gumbo.

If you are a Gumbo fan, you will love it.

Serves 12

Louisiana Gumbo
♥ MAG'S FAV

Start/Finish 2 1/2 hrs

1 5lb chicken, cut into pieces.
1 tsp garlic powder
1 tsp seasoned salt
1 tsp black pepper

1c vegetable oil

2 1/2 qt. water

3/4 c flour (all purpose)
1 celery stalk, chopped
3 med. onions, chopped
2 cloves garlic, chopped finely
1 bell pepper, chopped

1 lg. can diced stewed tomatoes
1 pkg. frozen okra or 2 c. fresh okra sliced
finely
1 pkg. frozen gumbo veggies

2 lbs peeled shrimp

1/2 lb smoked sausage, sliced thin (optional)
1 pt. fresh oysters (optional)

Season chicken pieces w/garlic powder, seasoned salt & pepper.

Heat oil & brown seasoned chicken in a lg frying pan. Set frying pan aside (Do not wash).

Move chicken to an 8 qt stockpot. Add water. Bring to a boil. Reduce heat & simmer 1 hr. Reserve the stock.

Remove & debone chicken. (Chop veggies now) Set frying pan aside (Do not wash).

Add flour, celery, onions, garlic & bell peppers to the frying pan. Making a roux (stir flour constantly until the flour turns brown & the veggies are tender)

Add Roux, water, tomatoes, frozen veggies & chicken meat to stock.

Cook about 30 min or until veggies are tender. Add shrimp.

Cook about 5 min (until the shrimp are pink). Add sausage & oysters, if desired, until heated thoroughly.

Serve over rice w/gumbo filé if desired.

This is the "Real Deal." You can even serve it to a Cajun. Maggie sometimes adds fresh crabmeat to it.

Quite a treat!

Serves 8

New England Clam Chowder

Start/Finish 45 min

> 1/4 c onions, chopped
> 2 Tbsp olive oil
>
> 2 c boiling water
> 2 c potatoes, diced
> 1 1/2 tsp salt
>
> 2 7oz cans minced clams w/juice
> 2 c whole milk or half & half thinned slightly
> thinned w/water
>
> Parsley
> Sherry

Place onions & oil in 4 qt saucepan. Cook until transparent, but not brown.

Add water, salt & potatoes. Cook until potatoes are tender (approx. 30 min).

Add clams & juice. Add milk slowly. Stir constantly until heated thru.

Let stand for several minutes to blend flavors.

Season to taste.

Ladle into bowls. Top with parsley & a dash of sherry, if desired.

This is one of husband Tim's favorite soups. He became addicted to it on a visit to Boston.

Serves 4

Old Fashion Beef Stew

Start/Finish 3 hrs

> 1/3 c flour (all purpose)
> 1 1/2 tsp salt
> Pinch of black pepper
>
> 1 1/2 lbs beef stew meat
>
> 2 Tbsp olive oil
> 2 1/4 c water
>
> 3 med onions, sliced
> 4 med potatoes, cut into cubes
> 5 med carrots, cut into quarters
>
> 1 1/2 c frozen peas

Combine flour, salt & pepper.

Coat cubes of beef with mixture.

Add oil to lg skillet. Brown meat thoroughly. Sprinkle remaining seasoned flour over meat. Stir well.

Add water, cover & simmer until meat is tender (approx 2 1/2 hrs.).

Add onions, potatoes & carrots. Recover & simmer for another 15 min.

Add peas & simmer until veggies are tender. (Approx 25 min). Stir occasionally.

Just reading this recipe makes me warm inside. Every time I make stew I have to try to remember what goes in stew. Anything and everything can go in stew. Play with it until you find your perfect combo.

Serves 6

Southwestern Tortellini Chowder

Start/Finish 20 min

> 3 10 1/2 oz cans chicken broth
> 1 1/2 c mild picante sauce
> 1/2 tsp orange peel, grated
>
> 2 9 oz pkg refrigerated meat or cheese filled tortellini
> 1 1lb pkg frozen corn, broccoli & red peppers
>
> 1 5oz can evaporated milk
> Dash of salt
>
> 1/4 c fresh cilantro, chopped

In a 6 qt stockpot combine broth, salsa & orange peel. Bring to a boil. Reduce heat & simmer 3 min.

Stir in tortellini & veggies. Cook over med heat until tortellini & veggies are tender (approx 6-8 min).

Stir in milk & salt. Cook 1 to 2 more min until heated thoroughly. Stir occasionally. (Do Not Boil).

Spoon into bowls & top with cilantro.

Cross between Italian & Mexican food. Surprisingly good combo.

Serves 6

Sweet Corn Chowder

Start/Finish 30 min

1 tsp olive oil
1 onions, chopped
2 c frozen hash brown potatoes, cubed
2 14 1/2 oz cans chicken broth

1 tsp salt
3/4 tsp onion powder
1/2 tsp garlic powder
1/2 tsp thyme, dried
1/2 tsp dry mustard
1/4 tsp paprika
1/4 tsp marjoram
3 1/2 c frozen white corn kernels
4 strips of bacon, cooked & crumbled
1 tsp Worcestershire sauce
2 dashes of hot pepper sauce (optional)

1/2 cup half & half (or whole milk)

Heat oil in 6 qt stockpot. Add onions & potatoes until they start to brown & stick (approx 3 min)

Stir occasionally. Add 1 can chicken broth & stir to remove bits from bottom of pot.

Add 2nd can of broth & all remaining ingredients except half & half. Bring to a boil.
Reduce heat to med. Cook covered for 12 min. Stir occasionally.

Add half & half. Recover & cook 1 min.

This is wonderful chowder, but if you want to please you family or friends even more, cut corn off the cob of sweet white corn when it is in season. Wow!!

Serves 6

CHILI

If you know our bio,
we are Texans.
If you ever lived in Texas
you know, once a Texan always a Texan.
This being said, we contend that
Texas has the BEST CHILI.
However,
in an attempt to be fair,
we collected a few chili recipes
from other areas of the country.
If we must be honest, they
are pretty darn good. Actually,
they are great. Try them all.

Enjoy!

Cincinnati Beef & Pork Chili

Start/Finish 45 min

2 lb beef, ground round
1 1/2 lbs boneless pork butt, cut into 1/2 in.
cubes

1 lg onion, chopped
1-2 jalapeno peppers, seeded & minced
2 cloves garlic, crushed

1 28oz can crushed tomatoes
1 12oz can beer (your preference)
1/2 c water
2 pkg chili seasoning mix
1/2 tsp allspice, ground
1/2 tsp cinnamon, ground

1 Tbsp salt
1 pkg (1 lb) bow tie pasta

1 c sharp cheddar cheese, shredded

Brown ground beef in a 6 qt stockpot. Remove beef with a slotted spoon to a lg bowl. Add pork to pot. Cook until pork is evenly browned (5 min). Remove pork with slotted spoon. Put in bowl w/beef.

Add onion, jalapenos & garlic to pot. Cook until onions are tender (3 min). Return beef & pork to pot.

Add tomatoes, beer, water, chili mix, all spice & cinnamon. Bring to a boil. Reduce heat to med.

Cook 45 min stirring occasionally.

Cook pasta w/salt per direction on pkg.

Serve chili over pasta. Sprinkle with cheese.

Different than regular Chili. It is sweet w/a bite!

Serves 10

Chunky Veggie Chili

Start/Finish 2 hrs

2 Tbsp olive oil
1 roasted pepper
1 c onions, diced
1 c carrots, diced
1 c bell peppers, diced
1 jalapeno, seeded & minced
1 med potato, diced
1 clove of garlic, minced

1 Tbsp chili powder
1 Tbsp cumin

1 11 oz can whole kernel corn
1 28 oz can crushed tomatoes
2 15 oz can chili beans
1 15 oz can kidney beans, drained
1/2 tsp red pepper flakes
3 c water

1 c uncooked rice

Heat oil in 6 qt stockpot. Add pepper, onions, carrots, bell pepper, jalapeno, potato & garlic. Sauté 7-10 min.

Add chili powder & cumin. Cook 3 min. Stir frequently.

Add corn, tomatoes, chili beans, kidney beans & red pepper. Stir to mix well. Add water. Bring to a boil.

Reduce heat to med. Simmer 45 min to 1 hr.

Cook rice according to directions. Set aside.

Add rice to cooked chili. Mix well. Season to taste.

This one is full of meat & veggie goodness. It's a different texture, but a similar taste to traditional chili.

Serves 8

Jenn's Game Day Chili

Finish 8 hrs or overnight

1 1/2 lbs ground beef (<90% lean recommended).

1/2 white onion
1/2 green pepper
1 Tbsp chili powder
1 tsp garlic salt

1 28 oz can chili beans
1 28 oz can diced stewed tomatoes
1 10oz can mild stewed tomatoes with green chilies
1 46 oz bottle spicy tomato/vegetable juice (may not use all)

Brown meat in a lg skillet. Add onion, pepper, chili powder & garlic salt.

While this is browning, start chili sauce in an 8 qt stockpot. Place beans, tomatoes (both) & half of the juice. Bring to a boil. Reduce heat & simmer.

Once beef is done, drain grease & add to pot.

Simmer 8-10 hrs. Stir occasionally. Add a little more juice if it gets too thick. It takes this long for pot & let it cook on low overnight.

Great Idea: get another can of tomatoes & a 2 lb box of processed cheese. Melt the 2 in the microwave. You can use them for dipping tortilla chips, but it is also fantastic in the chili & gives your family something to munch on while waiting on the chili.

Serves 8

Meaty Hot Dog Chili

Start/Finish 15 min

1 lb ground beef

1 c water
2 Tbsp chili powder
1 tsp garlic powder

Pinch of cayenne pepper
1/4 tsp salt
1/4 tsp ground black pepper

Hot Dogs & buns

Sharp cheddar cheese
Onions, chopped

Brown beef in med skillet. Add water, chili powder & garlic powder. Bring to a boil. Reduce heat & cook for 5 min. Remove from heat. Blend w/hand held blender or food processor. Grind until very fine.

Add cayenne, salt & pepper. Bring to a boil. Reduce heat & simmer until all water is evaporated.

Plate hot dogs in buns. Cover hot dogs with chili. Top with cheese & onions.

This makes enough chili for 8 hotdogs. Easy to double for a crowd.

Serves 8 *if everyone only eat one dog.*

Oven Baked Chili

Start/Finish 3-6 hrs

6 lbs ground beef, chuck
3 lg onions, chopped

4 garlic cloves, chopped fine
3 Tbsp chili powder
1 tsp cayenne pepper
2 Tbsp salt
2 Tbsp cumin, ground
1 Tbsp vinegar
2 1/2 qt water

Brown meat & onions in a 6 qt oven safe pot.

Add remaining ingredients. Cook uncovered in a 300° oven for 3 hrs or 200° oven for 5-6 hrs.

So easy to make that it almost made it into our Quick & Easy book.

Serves 10-12

Pork Chili with Black-Eyed Peas

Start/Finish 25 min

1 Tbsp vegetable oil
1/2 lb andouille sausage, chopped

1 lb ground pork

2 ribs of celery from the heart w/leaves
1 green bell pepper, chopped
1 onion, chopped
2 cloves garlic, chopped
1 bay leaf

2 c chicken broth
1 14 1/2 oz can stewed tomatoes, diced
1 15oz can black-eyed peas, drained
2 Tbsp hot pepper sauce
Dash of thyme, ground
2 Tbsp chili powder
1 Tbsp paprika
2 tsp coriander, ground

Scallions, chopped

Heat oil in 6 qt stockpot. Add sausage & cook until browned (approx 2 min).

Add ground pork & cook until browned & crumbly (approx 2 min).

Add celery, bell peppers, onion, garlic & bay leaf.

Cook, stirring occasionally, until the veggies soften (approx 5 min). Season to taste.

Stir in remaining ingredients except scallions. Bring to a low boil. Reduce heat & cook for 10 more min.

Ladle into bowls & top with scallions.

Serve with corn muffins.

Another good option for New Year's Day.

Serves 4

Squash & Black Bean Chili

Start/Finish 45 min

4 Tbsp vegetable oil
4 med yellow onions, chopped
2 med red bell peppers, seeded & chopped
2 med jalapeno, seeded & chopped fine

4 cloves of garlic, minced

2 c yellow squash, sliced
2 c zucchini squash, sliced
2 c vegetable or chicken broth
2 14 1/2 oz cans diced stewed tomatoes
2 15oz cans black beans, rinsed & drained
4 Tbsp chili powder
4 tsp cumin, ground
2 tsp oregano, dried
2 tsp salt

2 c corn, fresh or frozen

1 c cashews, chopped

Heat oil in an 8 qt stockpot. Add onions, peppers & jalapenos. Sauté until softened. Stir frequently.

Add garlic & cook for 1 min stirring constantly.

Add squash, broth, tomatoes, beans, chili powder, cumin, oregano & salt. Stir to combine. Bring to a boil.

Reduce heat, cover & simmer for 30 min. Stir occasionally.

Add corn & cook for 5 min. Stir occasionally.

Ladle into bowls. Top with cashews.

This makes for a great vegetarian option.

It would also make a great side dish.

Serves 6-8

True Texas Chili
♥ MAG'S FAV

Start/Finish 2 hrs

3 lbs lean ground beef
1 cloves of garlic, minced
1 sm yellow onion, minced

1 pt water
1 8 oz can tomato sauce
3/4 c chili powder
1 1/2 tsp salt
2 Tbsp cumin, ground
1 tsp oregano
1 tsp cayenne pepper
1 tsp paprika

Onion, chopped
Cheddar cheese, shredded
Sour cream

Brown meat w/garlic & onion in lg skillet (cook till gray not well done).

Add remaining ingredients. Bring to a boil. Reduce heat & simmer 1 1/2 to 2 hrs.

For a spicier version just up your red pepper.

Ladle into crocks. Top with chopped onions, shredded cheddar cheese & sour cream. Serve with tortilla chips, tortillas or corn bread.

For those of you that want to mess with "True TX Chili" you can add chili beans.

Play w/this recipe to find your favorite version.

You can add canned tomatoes or tomatoes with green chilies if you want more spice.

You can add 1/2 tsp of marjoram for a smoky taste.

If you like thicker chili, you can add 1/4 c masa powder at the end.

Serves 6

White Chicken Chili

Start/Finish 1 hr

2 lbs chicken tenders
1 tsp olive oil

1 pkg chili seasoning mix
3/4 c water

1 lg yellow onion, chopped
1 12oz can of chicken broth
1 4oz can of chopped green chilies (optional)
1 15oz can of white kidney beans

Shredded Monterrey jack cheese
Green onions, chopped

Heat lg frying pan. Add oil & chicken tenders. Brown chicken.

Add chili seasoning & water. Bring to a boil. Lower heat to med, cover & cook for 30 min (until chicken is tender).

Remove & shred chicken.

Return chicken to pan. Stir in onions, chicken broth, green chilies & beans. Return to a boil. Lower heat & simmer, covered for 15 min. If the mixture becomes too thick, add more chicken broth.

Ladle into bowls. Top with cheese & onions. Serve with tortilla chips or flour tortillas.

Over cornbread would be another excellent option. Nice alternative to beef chili.

Serves 6-8

Get 5 bonus desert recipes!
Just use your computer and type
http://www.VelocityHouseCooking.com/soups
into your browser for
free instant access

About The Author

Maggie & Brooke are a mother/daughter team who love to cook. Maggie has been planning parties and cooking for crowds for all of Brooke's life. Brooke followed suit by becoming a caterer and event planner with a hospitality degree. These Texas born women now live in Atlanta, Georgia. You will notice in their recipes a spicy southwestern style with a hint of southern charm. They cook and work together on a daily basis. Each of their recipes has been tested in their homes or the homes of friends & family. They are very hopeful that you love the recipes that they have added to this cookbook collection. Be on the lookout for more recipes to come.
For the **LOVE OF COOKING!**

Visit our Website
http://www.loveofcookingonline.com
Visit us at Amazon's Author Central
Author Central

Check out our books:
Love of Cooking: Volume I:
Amazing Appetizer Recipes
Amazing Side Dish Recipes
Simple Salad Recipes
Easy Soup Recipes
Marvelous Main Dishes
Love of Cooking: Volume II:
Easy Chicken Recipes
Simple Beef Recipes
Love of Cooking: Holiday Series:
Love of Cooking: 4th of July
Love of Cooking: Labor Day
Thanksgiving Recipes
Easy Christmas Recipes

INDEX

Printed in Great Britain
by Amazon

49912171R00058